Emotionally Spent

A 90-Day Guided Journal
To Help You Cope With The
Painful Side Effects Of Debt

Lindsay Snowden

Published By: Plan Then Buy, LLC

First Printing 2017

Graphic Design By: Alexa Marra Malonzo

ISBN-10: 1974633659

ISBN-13: 978-1974633654

www.EmotionallySpent.com

Matthew, your constant support and encouragement throughout this project adds to the already long list of reasons I love you.

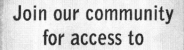

Get Your Free

Monthly Budget Workbook Here!

Printable Workbook Includes:

✓ Expense Activities

✓ Monthly Budget Planner

✓ Debt Tracker

To Download Go To:

www.EmotionallySpent.com/free

Bonus Resources

Visit www.EmotionallySpent.com/free to download your FREE *Monthly Budget Workbook* which includes: expense activities, a monthly budget planner and a debt tracker.

Do you want to know how to create a cash envelope system? Watch our videos at www.EmotionallySpent.com/pay-cash.

Does the grocery store stress you out? Get my *Grocery Store Planner* at www.EmotionallySpent.com/grocery-store.

Visit www.EmotionallySpent.com/generate-cash to see examples of items we have sold as well as used items we purchased online and at garage sales.

Visit www.EmotionallySpent.com/gifts to download my *Gift Giving Planner.*

To see examples of items we used negotiation tactics to purchase, visit www.EmotionallySpent.com/negotiate.

Visit www.EmotionallySpent.com for more resources and support!

Table of Contents

Foreword

Sticks and bricks *can* build great buildings and bridges in the hands of a skilled craftsman or become deathtraps in the hands of the untrained. A craftsman becomes skilled by watching, training, and doing as they observe those with experience. No amount of wishing and praying will turn those sticks and bricks into something useful until someone gets their hands dirty doing work.

The author, who happens to also be my beautiful and loving wife, Lindsay Snowden, has hard-earned every skillful exercise and resultant ground won that's shared in this journal. Based on her life experience, you will be well-served listening to her insight. Lindsay was forced to get her hands dirty dealing with debt (mostly mine).

Intellectually, I knew about financial sticks and bricks, but without adequate skills, I built an unsound financial house. Lindsay moved in, saw the cracking foundation, and knew we needed to shore things up before experiencing a total failure of our finances, marriage, and lives.

This journal transforms her wisdom into tools necessary for actually dealing with debt. Lindsay provides approachable, practical tools for dealing with the under-explored realities of our emotions relative to debt. We all need this tool. Lindsay empathizes and understands emotions as a mother, wife, daughter, friend, woman, entrepreneur, employee, and teacher. She has undertaken the painstaking process of turning homegrown, extraordinary tools into something beneficial.

Thank you Lindsay, and well done. Reader, whether this is for you or a loved one, don't think twice. This journal, and the time invested in completing it, represents only a tiny fraction of the financial, emotional, and relational toll that untamed debt took on us. We all need this tool along with Lindsay's insight to help us become "emotionally unspent".

Matthew Snowden

Welcome

In 2010, I married Matt, the love of my life. We were so excited to begin our life together and everything seemed to be perfect. What we didn't realize was that we were about to crash and burn financially. Shortly after our wedding, the housing market collapsed and we found ourselves facing an overwhelming amount of debt. We spent three years living on a tight budget, paying off debt, and fighting for our marriage through this stressful process. By the grace of God, we fought our way out of debt. We now live completely debt free, continue to live below our means, and our marriage is stronger than ever.

What surprised me the most about our journey out of debt was how hard it was on us emotionally. Well, how hard it was on ME emotionally. Matt has an amazing ability to compartmentalize his emotions, but I have a really hard time doing so. For me, it was more than creating a budget and crunching numbers. It required gaining the emotional strength necessary to say no to the things we couldn't afford and resisting the urge to be jealous of others. I spent many nights crying and wondering how we would ever get through our giant mess. While I despaired over our dwindling bank accounts, I found journaling about my thoughts and feelings brought me relief and was key to maintaining my emotional health during this exhausting process.

I created this journal to assist you with the emotional side of debt so you, too, would have a safe, personal place to express your emotions as you navigate your financial journey. I highly recommend seeking professional support through this process as well. I am not a licensed professional; I am simply providing a resource that I believe will help you through your journey.

Emotionally Spent does not teach you how to get out of debt. However, I have bonus resources available on my website (www.EmotionallySpent.com) that will provide you with additional support. There are amazing debt-fighting resources available, so take the time to research your options and pick the ones that suit you best. We completed Dave Ramsey's Financial Peace University through our church Living Streams and it was a great fit for us. My hope is that you will find the perfect resource for your situation to accompany *Emotionally Spent*.

All My Best,

Lindsay Snowden

Disclaimer: *Although the author has made every effort to ensure that the information in this book was correct at press time, the author does not assume, and hereby disclaims, any liability to any party for any loss, damage, or disruption caused by statements, errors and or omissions, whether such statements, errors or omissions result from negligence, accident, or any other cause.*

This book is not intended as a substitute for the financial and/or mental health advice of licensed professionals. The reader should regularly consult a licensed professional in matters relating to his/her financial and mental health and particularly with respect to any symptoms that may require diagnosis or medical attention as needed.

Introduction

My intent with *Emotionally Spent* is to provide you with a resource as you navigate your finances. When we were struggling to get out of debt, I noticed something very interesting: there are resources available explaining how to build a budget and how to pay off debt, but not many of them discuss the emotional toll that debt takes on a person. I often thought, "Am I really the only person out there who cringes when they hear the word budget?" I brought this up to my counselor and he suggested that I journal through this process and man, oh man, did it help.

My journal was a lifesaver; a place I could safely express my emotions and safely get everything off my chest. I found this to be very therapeutic and a huge component in our journey to become debt free. I knew that I couldn't possibly be the only person out there who struggled with their emotions while sorting through debt, so *Emotionally Spent* was born.

This 90-day guided journal consists of setting goals, completing weekly challenges, and thoughtfully responding to daily, weekly, and monthly questions. Some days you will cry, while other days you will laugh. Life is filled with ups and downs, and writing about them is important. There is something so healing about putting a pen to paper and letting your thoughts flow. I hope that you find this resource to be both gratifying and beneficial to your emotional well-being. There is no right or wrong time of day to journal, just commit to doing it every day.

Are you ready to get started?

Good. Let's do this!

Guided Journal User Guide

Welcome to the guided journal portion of *Emotionally Spent*. Over the next twelve weeks you will be equipped to explore and better understand your emotions through the powerful tool of journaling. I wish you all the best, and I hope *Emotionally Spent* empowers you to confront the emotional side of debt.

Weekly Challenge: Each week starts with a challenge. These challenges are derived from my personal struggles and victories as we fought to become debt free.

Daily Questions: You will explore the emotions that surround your finances by answering daily questions. Along with these daily questions, you will find a *Notes* section where you can jot down your thoughts as well as an emoji scale where you can rate how you are feeling each day (see below).

Daily Spending: Each day you can log your spending in three areas: cash, debit and credit. This is a great way to track your spending habits (see below).

Weekly Spending: At the end of each week you can total up your daily spending logs. This will quickly show you how much you spend each week (see below).

Weekly Wrap-Up: You will wrap up each week by answering questions about your week as well as set goals for the week ahead.

Monthly Check-In: At the end of every four weeks you will answer questions about the past month as well as set goals for the next four weeks. This is a great way to revisit the past and plan for the future.

Pro Tip: Throughout this journal, I have provided links to outside resources that will provide you with additional support.

Set Goals

When Matt and I started our journey toward getting out of debt, we decided to set goals for our family. We felt that if we set realistic and actionable goals we could successfully eliminate our debt. I highly encourage you to do the same for yourself.

If you are married or in a relationship, I suggest setting these goals with your significant other so you are both aligned on this journey. However, I do realize that you may have a significant other who is unwilling to participate in the process, so go ahead and set these goals independent of him/her. My hope is they will see a change in you and want to be a part of the process. Don't give up hope for them!

Answer the following questions. The more specific, the better!

1. What is the goal for my current debt?

2. I will put _____ in my saving's account each month.

3. I will put _____ in my emergency fund each month.

4. I will put _____ in my dream fund (vacation, car, house, etc.) each month.

5. In what ways do you want to change how you feel emotionally about your finances?

6. What changes do you want to see in your spending over the next thirty days?

7. Where do you want to see your finances in six months?

8. Where do you want to see your finances in a year?

9. List other financial goals you have.

Week One: Let Go

One of the hardest parts of getting out of debt is realizing that you need to let some things go. When we first sat down to create our budget we were shocked by how much we were spending each month. We wrote all our expenses down and then took those expenses to the chopping block. It was difficult to cut some things out of our budget, but once we were finished we were amazed by how much we were going to save each month.

Listed below are possible items you can cut from your monthly spending. This isn't easy, but it is necessary in order to reduce your monthly spending. Trust me, it is worth it!

Examples:

•Memberships (gym, magazines, online, retail, movies, etc.)

•Cable TV

•Eating out/happy hour

•Toys

•Pet expenses (toys, treats, bones, grooming, etc.)

•Vacations

•Manicures/pedicures

•Morning coffee run

Pro Tip: Visit www.EmotionallySpent.com/free to download your FREE *Monthly Budget Workbook* which includes: expense activities, a monthly budget planner and a debt tracker. This is a great way to prioritize what items stay and what items go from your spending.

Weekly Challenge #1

Answer the following questions:

1. Look at your monthly spending. What are three items that you can cut from your spending?

2. Can you eliminate more than three items? If so, list them below.

3. How much money will you save by not purchasing these items?

4. Do you think you will miss these items? Why? Will you still miss them in six months?

Notes

Daily Spending

Cash Debit Credit Total Daily Spending

Monday

1. After the weekend, I feel _____ because _____.

2. My goal for this week is _____.

3. Today I am thankful for _____.

4. Today I am frustrated with _____.

Today I Feel:

Notes

Daily Spending

| Cash | Debit | Credit | Total Daily Spending |

Tuesday

1. What was hard about today?

2. My goal for tomorrow is _____.

3. What items did you purchase today?

4. I can save money if _____.

Today I Feel:

Notes

Daily Spending

Cash   Debit   Credit   Total Daily Spending

Date _____/_____/_____

Wednesday

1. I saved _____ today because I chose not to buy _____.

2. I wish I could buy _____.

3. I am worried about _____.

4. I am hopeful about _____.

Today I Feel:

Notes

Daily Spending

Cash	Debit	Credit	Total Daily Spending

Thursday

1. _____ made me feel happy today.

2. I am feeling jealous of _____ today.

3. _____ is motivating me.

4. I have a bad habit of _____.

Today I Feel:

Notes

Daily Spending

Friday

1. I want to buy _____ this weekend.

2. How do you feel about your financial situation today?

3. What are you proud of yourself for today?

4. What is your hope for the weekend?

Today I Feel:

Notes

Daily Spending

Saturday

1. What is something you did this week that you are proud of?

2. Is there something you could have done better this week?

3. Overall, how do you feel about your financial journey so far?

4. One way I can save money this week is _____.

Today I Feel:

Notes

Daily Spending

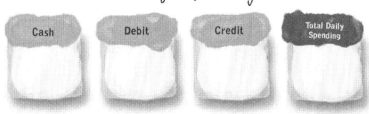

Sunday

1. My main frustrations from last week are _____.

2. Write out your celebrations from last week.

3. I am feeling optimistic about _____.

4. This week I am willing to give up _____ to save _____.

Today I Feel:

Weekly Wrap-Up

1. The following bills are due this coming week.

2. I get paid _____ this week.

3. My goals for this coming week are _____.

4. Were you able to successfully cut items from your budget?

5. Was it hard to let go of these items? Why or why not?

Week Two: Pay Cash

As I mentioned in the introduction of this book, Matt and I completed Dave Ramsey's Financial Peace University through our church in 2010. If you've heard of Dave Ramsey, you know he recommends paying cash for everything, so that's exactly what we did. We took this very seriously and had over thirty cash envelopes. We sat down each month, put money in our envelopes, and lived strictly on a cash budget...for three years!

Slowly but surely we became disciplined and only spent what we had, nothing more. This process took time to master, but once we did, spending within our budget became effortless. We had a system that worked for us and it set healthy boundaries for our spending.

To this day, I still have a cash envelope for our food budget. I am regularly tempted at the grocery store and having a cash envelope prevents me from overspending.

Answer the following questions:

1. In what ways have you explored Dave Ramsey's approach to the cash envelope system or something similar?

2. What items do you purchase with cash? What items do you purchase with cards?

Pro Tip: To learn more about our experience with Dave Ramsey's Financial Peace University visit (www.EmotionallySpent.com/DR).

3. List five areas where paying only with cash will help.

4. How much money do you think you will save by paying with cash in these areas?

Weekly Challenge #1:

My challenge for you is to choose three areas that you will spend cash only this week. You can choose what they are, but I strongly encourage you to make food one of them (yes, this includes coffee). Go to the bank and withdraw your cash for the week!

Pro Tip: Do you want to know how to create a cash envelope system? Watch our videos at www.EmotionallySpent.com/pay-cash.

Notes

Daily Spending

Cash	Debit	Credit	Total Daily Spending

Monday

1. After the weekend, I feel _____ because _____.

2. My goal for this week is _____.

3. Today I am thankful for _____.

4. Today I am frustrated with _____.

Today I Feel:

Notes

Daily Spending

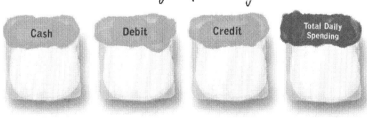

Tuesday

1. What was hard about today?

2. My goal for tomorrow is _____.

3. What items did you purchase today?

4. I can save money if _____.

Today I Feel:

Notes

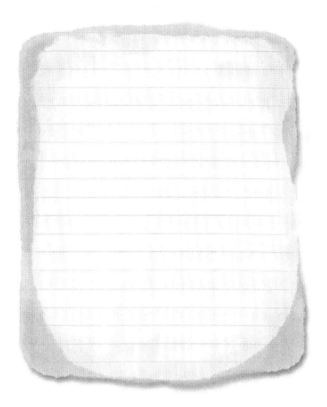

Daily Spending

Cash | Debit | Credit | Total Daily Spending

Wednesday

1. I saved _____ today because I chose not to buy _____.

2. I wish I could buy _____.

3. I am worried about _____.

4. I am hopeful about _____.

Today I Feel:

Notes

Daily Spending

Thursday

1. _____ made me feel happy today.

2. I am feeling jealous of _____ today.

3. _____ is motivating me.

4. I have a bad habit of _____.

Today I Feel:

Notes

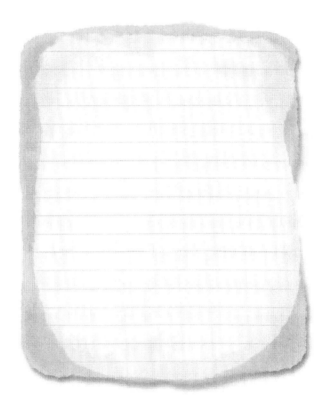

Daily Spending

Cash | Debit | Credit | Total Daily Spending

Friday

1. I want to buy _____ this weekend.

2. How do you feel about your financial situation today?

3. What are you proud of yourself for today?

4. What is your hope for the weekend?

Today I Feel:

Notes

Daily Spending

Cash   Debit   Credit   Total Daily Spending

Saturday

1. What is something you did that you are proud of this week?

2. Is there something you could have done better this week?

3. Overall, how do you feel about your financial journey so far?

4. One way I can save money this week is _____.

Today I Feel:

Notes

Daily Spending

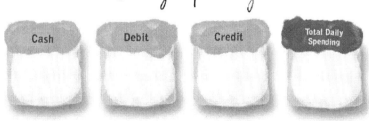

Sunday

1. My main frustrations from last week are _____.

2. Write out your celebrations from last week.

3. I am feeling optimistic about _____.

4. This week I am willing to give up _____ to save _____.

Today I Feel:

Weekly Wrap-Up

1. The following bills are due this coming week.

2. I get paid _____ this week.

3. My goals for this coming week are _____.

4. The weekly challenge was to choose three areas to use cash envelopes. Were you successful?

5. How did it feel using cash only in those three areas?

6. Why is it important for you to spend cash in those areas next week?

Week Three: Grocery Store Battle Plan

Every single time I go to the grocery store I prepare for battle. I always have three things: my grocery list, my envelope of cash, and a full stomach. *(We all know what happens when you are hungry at the store.)*

In order to maximize every single dollar, I build my menu for the week by looking through grocery store ads. While creating my menu, I look for recipes that have overlapping ingredients. For example: chicken, green peppers, garlic and onions are ingredients for both fajitas and chili. It is amazing how far you can stretch your food budget when ingredients overlap.

Next, I take my menu and make a list for each store I plan to visit. I have narrowed most of my monthly shopping down to three stores. One is where I buy bulk items, one has the cheapest produce and meat, and the third store is where I purchase canned or dry food items. While this takes a little more effort it saves my family money!

I pay cash at the grocery store in order to stick to my budget and prevent overspending. I know every single one of those end caps will be calling my name. Chocolate covered mangos? Yes, please! I grab them and then notice, $12.99. Oh man, seriously?! I put them back and grab the eggs, bread, and milk for the same price. One of these days I am going to go to the store wearing a football uniform and tackle all those end caps filled with expensive gourmet treats! Cash truly is my best friend at the grocery store as it prevents me from racking up a food bill that my family cannot afford.

Even if you don't like cooking as much as I do, the grocery store is a place where you should really pay attention. You will be amazed how much money you can save on food by simply being aware of your spending habits.

Pro Tip: Does the grocery store stress you out? Get my *Grocery Store Planner* at www.EmotionallySpent.com/grocery-store.

Challenge #1

My first challenge is for you to select **at least** five items that you will NOT purchase at the grocery store this week. List your items below:

1. Why will these items be hard for you to give up?

2. How much money will you save by not purchasing these items?

Challenge #2

My second challenge is for you to create your grocery store battle plan for this week. Create your menu, write your list, estimate how much you will spend, use cash instead of your credit card, and stick to your plan.

Notes

Daily Spending

Cash   Debit   Credit   Total Daily Spending

Monday

1. After the weekend, I feel _____ because _____.

2. My goal for this week is _____.

3. Today I am thankful for _____.

4. Today I am frustrated with _____.

Today I Feel:

Tuesday

1. What was hard about today?

2. My goal for tomorrow is _____.

3. What items did you purchase today?

4. I can save money if _____.

Today I Feel:

Notes

Daily Spending

Wednesday

1. I saved _____ today because I chose not to buy _____.

2. I wish I could buy _____.

3. I am worried about _____.

4. I am hopeful about _____.

Today I Feel:

Notes

Daily Spending

Thursday

1. _____ made me feel happy today.

2. I am feeling jealous of _____ today.

3. _____ is motivating me.

4. I have a bad habit of _____.

Today I Feel:

Notes

Daily Spending

Friday

1. I want to buy _____ this weekend.

2. How do you feel about your financial situation today?

3. What are you proud of yourself for today?

4. What is your hope for the weekend?

Today I Feel:

Notes

Daily Spending

Cash   Debit   Credit   Total Daily Spending

Saturday

1. What is something you did that you are proud of this week?

2. Is there something you could have done better this week?

3. Overall, how do you feel about your financial journey so far?

4. One way I can save money this week is _____.

Today I Feel:

Notes

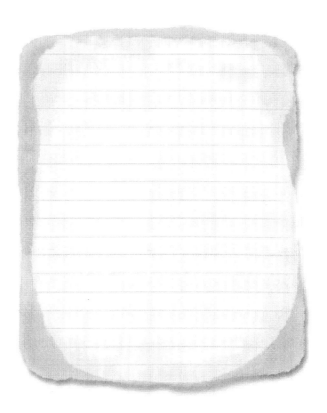

Daily Spending

Date ____/____/_____

Sunday

1. My main frustrations from last week are _____.

2. Write out your celebrations from last week.

3. I am feeling optimistic about _____.

4. This week I am willing to give up _____ to save _____.

Today I Feel:

Weekly Wrap-Up

1. The following bills are due this coming week.

2. I get paid _____ this week.

3. My goals for this coming week are _____.

4. Were you able to resist purchasing the five items you listed in this week's challenge?

5. How did it feel using your grocery store battle plan?

Week Four: Comparison

A difficult aspect of a financial transformation is the comparison death trap. I remember when we first cut our spending and started living out of cash envelopes. I was immediately overwhelmed with how I felt when comparing myself to others. This was a feeling that I had been unfamiliar with since I was used to getting what I wanted, when I wanted it. When I chose to stop using credit cards, I could no longer live like that. As Theodore Roosevelt said, "comparison is the thief of joy" and boy, oh boy, did I feel that every single day on my journey to becoming debt free.

I felt miserable when I went shopping with my friends. They swiped their cards freely and I would peek into my cash envelope that had a $30 cash limit and pick out a thing or two. Going out to lunch and dinner was also difficult. Instead of choosing freely from the menu, I would order water, skip the appetizer, and pick an inexpensive entrée. One summer I watched from afar as my friends took a trip to the beach. I wanted to go so badly, but I simply couldn't afford it. The hardest part was that they didn't understand why I couldn't go; they didn't understand that my new lifestyle of becoming debt free didn't allow me to swipe my card and land in the sand.

Through this process I began gaining strength. I was conditioning my body and mind, becoming stronger than I ever knew possible. Over time those envelopes that once caused me embarrassment filled me with pride. You see, what I realized was that when you live life spending only money you truly have, cash, then a burden starts lifting from your shoulders. My confidence grew as our pile of debt began disappearing. My foggy lens of comparing myself to others cleared up and I felt a sense of peace that I never knew was possible.

Weekly Challenge #1

Answer the following questions:

1. How do you compare yourself to others financially?

2. Can your friends, family and coworkers afford their lifestyle?

3. What are some ways you can stay on track financially when comparing yourself to others?

4. What is one item that you saw online, on social media or on TV that you know is completely unrealistic financially?

Notes

Daily Spending

Monday

1. After the weekend, I feel _____ because _____.

2. My goal for this week is _____.

3. Today I am thankful for _____.

4. Today I am frustrated with _____.

Today I Feel:

Notes

Daily Spending

Tuesday

1. What was hard about today?

2. My goal for tomorrow is _____.

3. What items did you purchase today?

4. I can save money if _____.

Today I Feel:

Notes

Daily Spending

Wednesday

1. I saved _____ today because I chose not to buy _____.

2. I wish I could buy _____.

3. I am worried about _____.

4. I am hopeful about _____.

Today I Feel:

Notes

Daily Spending

Cash	Debit	Credit	Total Daily Spending

Thursday

1. _____ made me feel happy today.

2. I am feeling jealous of _____ today.

3. _____ is motivating me.

4. I have a bad habit of _____.

Today I Feel:

Notes

Daily Spending

| Cash | Debit | Credit | Total Daily Spending |

Friday

1. I want to buy_____ this weekend.

2. How do you feel about your financial situation today?

3. What are you proud of yourself for today?

4. What is your hope for the weekend?

Today I Feel:

Notes

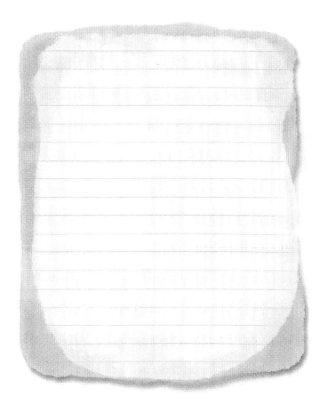

Daily Spending

Cash   Debit   Credit   Total Daily Spending

Saturday

1. What is something you did that you are proud of this week?

2. Is there something you could have done better this week?

3. Overall, how do you feel about your financial journey so far?

4. One way I can save money this week is _____.

Today I Feel:

Notes

Daily Spending

Date ____/____/_____

Sunday

1. My main frustrations from last week are _____.

2. Write out your celebrations from last week.

3. I am feeling optimistic about _____.

4. This week I am willing to give up _____ to save _____.

Today I Feel:

Weekly Wrap-Up

1. The following bills are due this coming week.

2. I get paid _____this week.

3. My goals for this coming week are _____.

4. Did you catch yourself falling into the comparison death trap this week? With whom? Why?

5. How did you overcome your feelings of comparison this week?

Monthly Check-In

1. List the bills that are due this month.

2. I am getting paid _____ this month.

3. My goal is to pay off _____ debt this month.

4. This month, I am willing to give up _____ to save _____.

5. If I did _____ instead of _____ I could save _____.

6. My goals for this month are _____.

Week Five: Generate Cash

One of our favorite options when we are short on cash is to sell stuff around our house. You can have a garage sale, post it online, or take it to a consignment shop. With very little effort you can create cash quickly. Here are some ideas of things you can sell:

- Furniture
- Toys
- Clothing
- TV, electronics, stereo, etc.
- Lamps
- Books
- DVDs/CDs
- Baby stuff
- Power tools
- Camera
- Bicycles
- Camping gear
- Appliances
- Exercise equipment
- Car, motorcycle, boat, motorhome
- Workout equipment

Weekly Challenge #1

Look around your house, what are at least ten items you can sell? List them below.

Weekly Challenge #2

List these items for sale. The sooner the better.

Tips for selling:

- Write a detailed description for each item. This will make your listing more desirable.
- Stage your items and take nice photos. Buyers will judge the quality based on the photo.
- Set your price slightly higher than you think it will sell for as this leaves room for negotiation and creates a higher perceived value.

Pro Tip: Visit www.EmotionallySpent.com/generate-cash to see examples of items we have sold as well as used items we purchased online and at garage sales.

Notes

Daily Spending

Monday

1. After the weekend, I feel _____ because _____.

2. My goal for this week is _____.

3. Today I am thankful for _____.

4. Today I am frustrated with _____.

Today I Feel:

Notes

Daily Spending

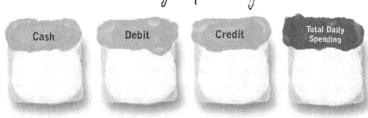

Cash   Debit   Credit   Total Daily Spending

Tuesday

1. What was hard about today?

2. My goal for tomorrow is _____.

3. What items did you purchase today?

4. I can save money if _____.

Today I Feel:

Notes

Daily Spending

Cash	Debit	Credit	Total Daily Spending

Wednesday

1. I saved _____ today because I chose not to buy _____.

2. I wish I could buy _____.

3. I am worried about _____.

4. I am hopeful about _____.

Today I Feel:

Notes

Daily Spending

Cash	Debit	Credit	Total Daily Spending

Thursday

1. _____ made me feel happy today.

2. I am feeling jealous of _____ today.

3. _____ is motivating me.

4. I have a bad habit of _____.

Today I Feel:

Notes

Daily Spending

Cash | Debit | Credit | Total Daily Spending

Friday

1. I want to buy _____ this weekend.

2. How do you feel about your financial situation today?

3. What are you proud of yourself for today?

4. What is your hope for the weekend?

Today I Feel:

Notes

Daily Spending

Cash · Debit · Credit · Total Daily Spending

Saturday

1. What is something you did that you are proud of this week?

2. Is there something you could have done better this week?

3. Overall, how do you feel about your financial journey so far?

4. One way I can save money this week is _____.

Today I Feel:

Notes

Daily Spending

| Cash | Debit | Credit | Total Daily Spending |

Sunday

1. My main frustrations from last week are _____.

2. Write out your celebrations from last week.

3. I am feeling optimistic about _____.

4. This week I am willing to give up _____ to save _____.

Today I Feel:

Weekly Wrap-Up

1. The following bills are due this coming week.

2. I get paid _____ this week.

3. My goals for this coming week are _____.

4. What items did you list for sale this week?

5. Did any of those items sell? How much cash did you generate?

Week Six: Be Creative

One month we were tight on cash. I really needed to go to the grocery store but there wasn't any room in our budget. I noticed all of our spare change sprawled out over the filing cabinet. I gathered it up, turned on the TV, and started rolling coins. I rolled coins for three hours and was surprised by how many quarters were hidden among the piles of pennies. When I finished, there was $106! That meant with very little effort I made $35/hour, sweet!

I proudly took those rolled coins to our bank and exchanged them for cash. *(Let's be real, I wasn't about to check out at the grocery store with piles of rolled coins.)* I took the cash to the grocery store and filled our fridge. That was one of the happiest shopping trips I've ever had. People probably thought I was crazy because I was smiling and telling everyone hello. I couldn't help it, a sense of accomplishment simply radiated from my body.

Answer the following questions:

1. How can some extra cash benefit you this week?

2. Do you have a pile of change lying around?

Pro Tip: Your bank will give you free rolls for your coins. So go to the bank, come home, and roll your coins while watching your favorite show or listening to your favorite podcast.

Weekly Challenge #1

Can you think of other creative ways to make money? List those ideas below and choose one you will do this week.

Please share your creative ideas with me and other readers at www.EmotionallySpent.com/community and with your friends and family on Facebook, Twitter or Instagram using @EmotionallySpent.

Notes

Daily Spending

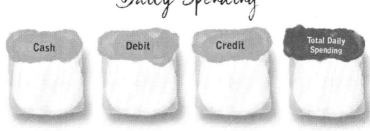

Monday

1. After the weekend, I feel _____ because _____.

2. My goal for this week is _____.

3. Today I am thankful for _____.

4. Today I am frustrated with _____.

Today I Feel:

Notes

Daily Spending

Tuesday

1. What was hard about today?

2. My goal for tomorrow is _____.

3. What items did you purchase today?

4. I can save money if _____.

Today I Feel:

Notes

Daily Spending

Cash	Debit	Credit	Total Daily Spending

Wednesday

1. I saved _____ today because I chose not to buy _____.

2. I wish I could buy _____.

3. I am worried about _____.

4. I am hopeful about _____.

Today I Feel:

Notes

Daily Spending

Thursday

1. _____ made me feel happy today.

2. I am feeling jealous of _____ today.

3. _____ is motivating me.

4. I have a bad habit of _____.

Today I Feel:

Notes

Daily Spending

Cash	Debit	Credit	Total Daily Spending

Friday

1. I want to buy _____ this weekend.

2. How do you feel about your financial situation today?

3. What are you proud of yourself for today?

4. What is your hope for the weekend?

Today I Feel:

Notes

Daily Spending

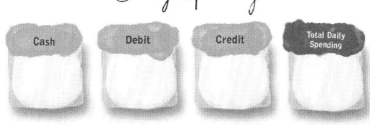

Saturday

1. What is something you did that you are proud of this week?

2. Is there something you could have done better this week?

3. Overall, how do you feel about your financial journey so far?

4. One way I can save money this week is _____.

Today I Feel:

Notes

Daily Spending

Cash | Debit | Credit | Total Daily Spending

Sunday

1. My main frustrations from last week are _____.

2. Write out your celebrations from last week.

3. I am feeling optimistic about _____.

4. This week I am willing to give up _____ to save _____.

Today I Feel:

Weekly Wrap-Up

1. The following bills are due this coming week.

2. I get paid _____ this week.

3. My goals for this coming week are _____.

4. How much money did you make from rolling coins this week?

5. Did you think of a creative way to make extra money?

Week Seven: Persistence

Myth: Overcoming debt is a one-time battle. Yeah right!! If you want to overcome debt and stay out of debt this is a lifetime battle folks! Yes, Matt and I are debt free, but we still battle to keep it that way. While it is hard at first, don't give up, it does get easier once you establish financial routines. The years that it took to become debt free taught us to be disciplined with every purchasing decision. Discipline is hard but worth it.

Your debt battles will be unique to you. Some people enjoy buying clothing, some enjoy fancy cars, others love to go out for happy hour. The grocery store is my weekly battleground because I love cooking. It is the one place where I know I need to be disciplined and can't buy everything I want.

There is not an exotic vacation, fancy car, or expensive outfit that will ever feel better than the day we yelled, "WE'RE DEBT FREE." The fight to becoming debt free is challenging but, there are small wins along the way that will motivate you. Just don't ever give up! Trust me, the last payment on that credit card, student loan, or car loan will make you feel like you are on top of the world!

Weekly Challenge #1

Answer the following questions:

1. Have you overcome debt before?

2. What is the hardest part of your current financial journey?

3. Where do you intend to see yourself financially in five years?

4. What debt-fighting programs have you explored? How are they serving you?

5. What dreams will be possible once you've conquered debt?

Notes

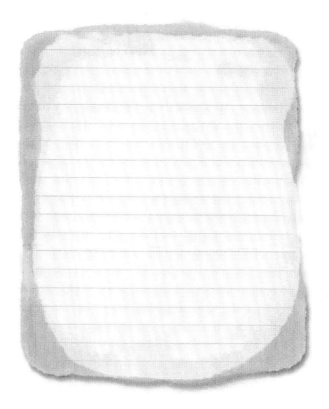

Daily Spending

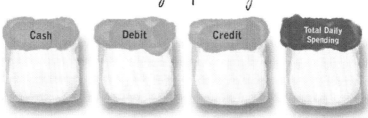

Date ____/____/_____

Monday

1. After the weekend, I feel _____ because _____.

2. My goal for this week is _____.

3. Today I am thankful for _____.

4. Today I am frustrated with _____.

Today I Feel:

Notes

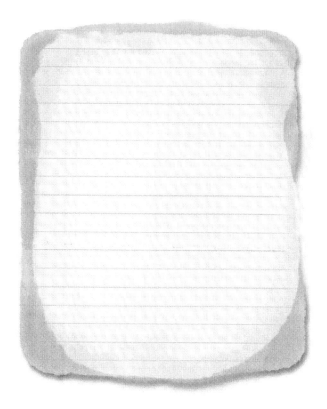

Daily Spending

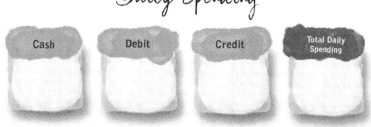

Cash   Debit   Credit   Total Daily Spending

Tuesday

1. What was hard about today?

2. My goal for tomorrow is _____.

3. What items did you purchase today?

4. I can save money if _____.

Today I Feel:

Notes

Daily Spending

Wednesday

1. I saved _____ today because I chose not to buy _____.

2. I wish I could buy _____.

3. I am worried about _____.

4. I am hopeful about _____.

Today I Feel:

Notes

Daily Spending

Thursday

1. _____ made me feel happy today.

2. I am feeling jealous of _____ today.

3. _____ is motivating me.

4. I have a bad habit of _____.

Today I Feel:

Notes

Daily Spending

Friday

1. I want to buy _____ this weekend.

2. How do you feel about your financial situation today?

3. What are you proud of yourself for today?

4. What is your hope for the weekend?

Today I Feel:

Notes

Daily Spending

Saturday

1. What is something you did that you are proud of this week?

2. Is there something you could have done better this week?

3. Overall, how do you feel about your financial journey so far?

4. One way I can save money this week is _____.

Today I Feel:

Notes

Daily Spending

Sunday

1. My main frustrations from last week are _____.

2. Write out your celebrations from last week.

3. I am feeling optimistic about _____.

4. This week I am willing to give up _____ to save _____.

Today I Feel:

Weekly Wrap-Up

1. The following bills are due this coming week.

2. I get paid _____ this week.

3. My goals for this coming week are _____.

4. How do you feel about your financial journey this week?

5. What debt-fighting programs did you explore this week?

6. What steps did you take towards your financial dreams this week?

Week Eight: Strategic Gift Giving

Cutting our gift giving budget was a difficult task. Not being able to provide my loved ones, co-workers, and friends with gifts for every imaginable occasion was tough. I find so much joy in selecting gifts, wrapping them, and watching faces light up when they are opened. I quickly realized that my envelope could no longer keep up with my desire to buy gifts for others.

What I wasn't expecting in return was that my gift receivers didn't stop loving me when I cut back on my gifts to them. The truth is, they wanted me to take care of myself and just a simple conversation filled them with the same joy. Over time, I realized I can show my love to them in different ways than a physical gift. It is still my hope that one day I will have plenty of expendable income and will be able to shower people in gifts once again. Until then, I will continue to reign in my spending and stick to my budget.

Pro Tip: Visit www.EmotionallySpent.com/gifts to download my *Gift Giving Planner.*

Weekly Challenge #1

Answer the following questions:

1. How much do you anticipate spending this year on gifts?

2. Why do you enjoy giving gifts?

3. Write out a list of people you will be giving gifts to this year. Please include holiday giving.

4. Think back on a time when you spent too much money on a gift? How did that make you feel?

5. List three things you can give without spending money.

6. Who can you share with about changing the way you give?

7. Is there someone who would benefit from receiving a copy of this book from you instead of a last minute panic gift?

Notes

Daily Spending

Monday

1. After the weekend, I feel _____ because _____.

2. My goal for this week is _____.

3. Today I am thankful for _____.

4. Today I am frustrated with _____.

Today I Feel:

Notes

Daily Spending

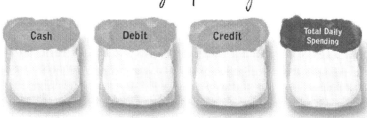

Tuesday

1. What was hard about today?

2. My goal for tomorrow is _____.

3. What items did you purchase today?

4. I can save money if _____.

Today I Feel:

Notes

Daily Spending

Wednesday

1. I saved _____ today because I chose not to buy _____.

2. I wish I could buy _____.

3. I am worried about _____.

4. I am hopeful about _____.

Today I Feel:

Notes

Daily Spending

Thursday

1. _____ made me feel happy today.

2. I am feeling jealous of _____ today.

3. _____ is motivating me.

4. I have a bad habit of _____.

Today I Feel:

Notes

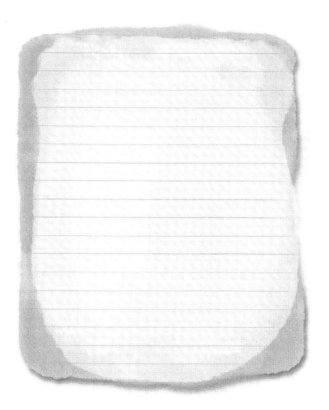

Daily Spending

Friday

1. I want to buy _____ this weekend.

2. How do you feel about your financial situation today?

3. What are you proud of yourself for today?

4. What is your hope for the weekend?

Today I Feel:

Notes

Daily Spending

Cash · Debit · Credit · Total Daily Spending

Saturday

1. What is something you did that you are proud of this week?

2. Is there something you could have done better this week?

3. Overall, how do you feel about your financial journey so far?

4. One way I can save money this week is _____.

Today I Feel:

Notes

Daily Spending

Sunday

1. My main frustrations from last week are _____.

2. Write out your celebrations from last week.

3. I am feeling optimistic about _____.

4. This week I am willing to give up _____ to save _____.

Today I Feel:

Weekly Wrap-Up

1. The following bills are due this coming week.

2. I get paid _____ this week.

3. My goals for this coming week are _____ .

4. What was difficult about making your gift giving list?

5. How did you go about creating a budget for gift giving?

Monthly Check-In

1. List the bills that are due this month.

2. I am getting paid _____ this month.

3. My goal is to pay off _____ debt this month.

4. This month, I am willing to give up _____ to save _____.

5. If I did _____ instead of _____ I could save _____.

6. My goals for this month are _____.

Week Nine: Forgive

As I mentioned in the introduction of this book, our journey out of debt was strenuous on our marriage. At first, my heart turned cold towards my husband when I realized how much debt we had. I seemed to have completely forgotten the promise I made to him sixty days prior. Two months earlier I stood at the altar, looked him in the eye, and promised him that I would love him in good times and bad. Somehow my hardened heart forgot all about those words.

Going to marriage counseling was not an easy process but it was necessary. It gave us a way to talk through our problems which, at the time, revolved around our finances. It softened my heart, helped me to love him unconditionally, and allowed me to forgive him for the debt he brought into our marriage. Without this forgiveness, our marriage wouldn't be the same. The power of forgiveness feels amazing.

This new-found forgiveness allowed us to realign emotionally and enabled us to tackle our debt at hand. We stood side-by-side and worked together to overcome our financial challenges. Without forgiveness, my heart would have stood in the way of our financial freedom.

Weekly Challenge #1

Everyone's situation is different. I want you to take a few minutes to explore who is causing you pain regarding your finances. List them below along with how they make you feel - including yourself!

Consider the following questions:

1. Who is the number one person - including yourself - causing you pain regarding your finances?

2. How might forgiving this individual - or yourself - impact your ability to overcome your debt?

3. What is standing in your way of forgiving them - or yourself?

4. How will life be different once you make the conscious decision to forgive them - or yourself?

Pro Tip: As I mentioned previously, my husband and I used a professional counselor to help with this process. I highly encourage you to do the same. It is worth the investment.

Notes

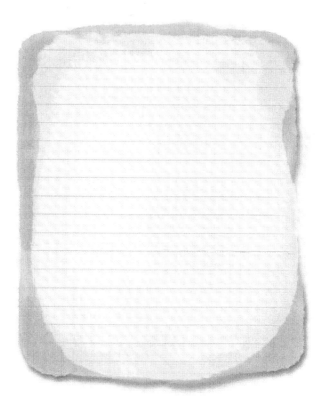

Daily Spending

Monday

1. After the weekend, I feel _____ because _____.

2. My goal for this week is _____.

3. Today I am thankful for _____.

4. Today I am frustrated with _____.

Today I Feel:

Notes

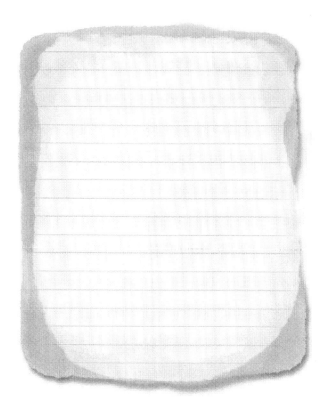

Daily Spending

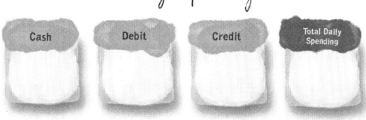

Tuesday

1. What was hard about today?

2. My goal for tomorrow is _____.

3. What items did you purchase today?

4. I can save money if _____.

Today I Feel:

Notes

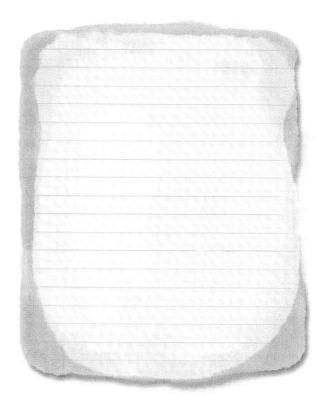

Daily Spending

Wednesday

1. I saved _____ today because I chose not to buy _____.

2. I wish I could buy _____.

3. I am worried about _____.

4. I am hopeful about _____.

Today I Feel:

Notes

Daily Spending

Cash | Debit | Credit | Total Daily Spending

Thursday

1. _____ made me feel happy today.

2. I am feeling jealous of _____ today.

3. _____ is motivating me.

4. I have a bad habit of _____.

Today I Feel:

Notes

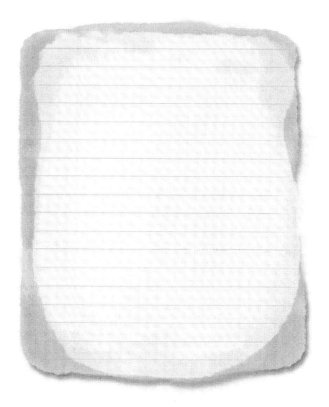

Daily Spending

Friday

1. I want to buy _____ this weekend.

2. How do you feel about your financial situation today?

3. What are you proud of yourself for today?

4. What is your hope for the weekend?

Today I Feel:

Notes

Daily Spending

Saturday

1. What is something you did that you are proud of this week?

2. Is there something you could have done better this week?

3. Overall, how do you feel about your financial journey so far?

4. One way I can save money this week is _____.

Today I Feel:

Notes

Daily Spending

Sunday

1. My main frustrations from last week are _____.

2. Write out your celebrations from last week.

3. I am feeling optimistic about _____.

4. This week I am willing to give up _____ to save _____.

Today I Feel:

Weekly Wrap-Up

1. The following bills are due this coming week.

2. I get paid _____ this week.

3. My goals for this coming week are _____.

4. How did you approach forgiveness this week? How did it feel?

5. Was this week's challenge difficult? Why or why not?

Week Ten: Negotiate

The price tag on most items that you purchase can be negotiated. Whether it is asking for a coupon at checkout, offering a lower price for an item, or paying cash, discounts always exist. My husband is the king of negotiating and encouraged me to learn how to successfully negotiate. His style of negotiating is quite the opposite of mine. I guess you could say he is the bad cop and I am the good cop; however, both styles seem to work. We like to feel out the situation and if it requires an assertive and persistent negotiation style I tag my husband in; if the situation requires a sweet loving voice, he tags me in.

We are a good team when we work together using our negotiation strengths. We even have key words that we use so that we don't lose our position of power with the sales representative. For instance, if I say, "I think that will work," Matt knows I really mean, "OH MY GOSH, I have to have it!" and the negotiations begin. Matt steps in and helps to assertively negotiate a great deal.

Pro Tip: The one style of negotiating that does not work is to be rude and mean. That never ever works so scratch that from your brain because there is no reason to hurt someone's feelings during this process. Look for a way both parties get what they want.

Answer the following questions:

1. How do you use negotiating for your purchases?

2. Does negotiating make you uncomfortable? Why or why not?

3. When was the last time you negotiated the price of an item?

4. How much money did you save?

Weekly Challenge #1

List a few items that you need to purchase this month that you will negotiate the price.

Pro Tip: To see examples of items we used negotiation tactics to purchase, visit www.EmotionallySpent.com/negotiate.

Notes

Daily Spending

Date ____/____/_____

Monday

1. After the weekend, I feel _____ because _____.

2. My goal for this week is _____.

3. Today I am thankful for _____.

4. Today I am frustrated with _____.

Today I Feel:

Notes

Daily Spending

Cash | Debit | Credit | Total Daily Spending

Tuesday

1. What was hard about today?

2. My goal for tomorrow is _____.

3. What items did you purchase today?

4. I can save money if _____.

Today I Feel:

Notes

Daily Spending

Wednesday

1. I saved _____ today because I chose not to buy _____.

2. I wish I could buy _____.

3. I am worried about _____.

4. I am hopeful about _____.

Today I Feel:

Notes

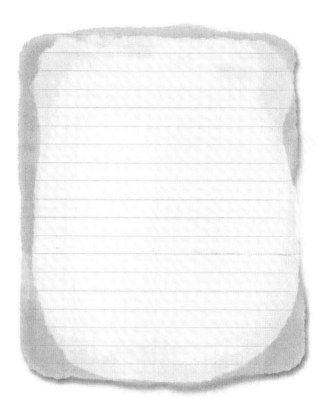

Daily Spending

Thursday

1. _____ made me feel happy today.

2. I am feeling jealous of _____ today.

3. _____ is motivating me.

4. I have a bad habit of _____.

Today I Feel:

Notes

Daily Spending

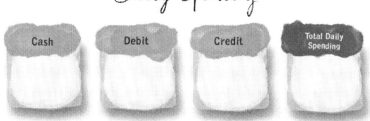

Cash | Debit | Credit | Total Daily Spending

Friday

1. I want to buy _____ this weekend.

2. How do you feel about your financial situation today?

3. What are you proud of yourself for today?

4. What is your hope for the weekend?

Today I Feel:

Notes

Daily Spending

Saturday

1. What is something you did that you are proud of this week?

2. Is there something you could have done better this week?

3. Overall, how do you feel about your financial journey so far?

4. One way I can save money this week is _____.

Today I Feel:

Notes

Daily Spending

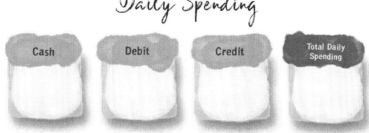

Cash | Debit | Credit | Total Daily Spending

Sunday

1. My main frustrations from last week are _____.

2. Write out your celebrations from last week.

3. I am feeling optimistic about _____.

4. This week I am willing to give up _____ to save _____.

Today I Feel:

Weekly Wrap-Up

1. The following bills are due this coming week.

2. I get paid _____ this week.

3. My goals for this coming week are _____.

4. How did you negotiate the price of an item this week? How much money did you save?

Please share your negotiation successes with me and other readers at www.EmotionallySpent.com/community or with your friends on Facebook, Twitter or Instagram using @EmotionallySpent.

Week Eleven: Seek Counseling

One item we always make sure we have money for is counseling. We have regularly been to a couple's counselor, individual counselors, and a financial advisor. When facing difficult times in life, it is so important to have support. Times like these are not meant to be dealt with alone. Seeking professional advice and support during times of despair is a key to successfully healing. Doing so does require you to humble yourself and reach out for help; however, once you do, freedom and peace fill your heart.

Our marriage counselors helped strengthen our marriage more than once. Life would have been very different without them. My counselor created a refuge for me, and my life would not be the same without her. Our financial advisor consistently helps us with tough and exciting financial decisions. We find it comforting to have someone walk along with us as we work through each decision.

Weekly Challenge #1

Answer the following questions:

1. How have you participated in counseling?

2. Who do you go to for professional counsel?

3. How do you feel about couple's counseling?

4. Who can you turn to for financial advice?

5. What are your thoughts about using a counselor.

6. List a few ways a counselor could help you.

7. Jot down a few questions that you might ask a financial advisor.

Notes

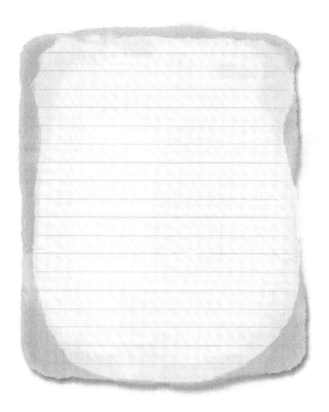

Daily Spending

Date _____/_____/_____

Monday

1. After the weekend, I feel _____ because _____.

2. My goal for this week is _____.

3. Today I am thankful for _____.

4. Today I am frustrated with _____.

Today I Feel:

Notes

Daily Spending

Cash | Debit | Credit | Total Daily Spending

Tuesday

1. What was hard about today?

2. My goal for tomorrow is _____.

3. What items did you purchase today?

4. I can save money if _____.

Today I Feel:

Notes

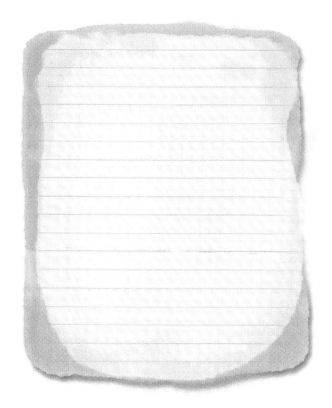

Daily Spending

Cash | Debit | Credit | Total Daily Spending

Wednesday

1. I saved _____ today because I chose not to buy _____.

2. I wish I could buy _____.

3. I am worried about _____.

4. I am hopeful about _____.

Today I Feel:

Notes

Daily Spending

Thursday

1. _____ made me feel happy today.

2. I am feeling jealous of _____ today.

3. _____ is motivating me.

4. I have a bad habit of _____.

Today I Feel:

Notes

Daily Spending

Friday

1. I want to buy _____ this weekend.

2. How do you feel about your financial situation today?

3. What are you proud of yourself for today?

4. What is your hope for the weekend?

Today I Feel:

Notes

Daily Spending

Cash · Debit · Credit · Total Daily Spending

Saturday

1. What is something you did that you are proud of this week?

2. Is there something you could have done better this week?

3. Overall, how do you feel about your financial journey so far?

4. One way I can save money this week is _____.

Today I Feel:

Notes

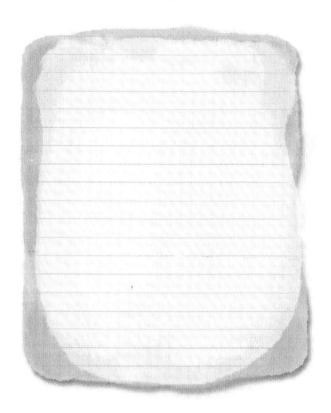

Daily Spending

Cash   Debit   Credit   Total Daily Spending

Sunday

1. My main frustrations from last week are _____.

2. Write out your celebrations from last week.

3. I am feeling optimistic about _____.

4. This week I am willing to give up _____ to save _____.

Today I Feel:

Weekly Wrap-Up

1. The following bills are due this coming week.

2. I get paid _____ this week.

3. My goals for this coming week are _____.

4. Did you consider finding a counselor? Why or why not?

5. Did you consider finding a financial advisor? Why or why not?

Week Twelve: Have Fun

One area that crushed our wallets was entertainment: restaurants, movies, throwing parties, staycations, vacations, etc. We quickly put an end to this expensive habit when we tightened our budget. We didn't give up on fun; instead, we got creative! We exchanged movies out with movies on the couch. We exchanged expensive restaurants with yummy home-cooked meals. Steaks at home are a fraction of the cost and are just as delicious. We turned parties into potlucks, it turns out that friends like to pitch in.

My husband just sent a text, as I am writing this, to see if we want to do dinner and game night at our neighbor's house tonight. Rather than paying for a babysitter, we will bring the pack-and-play and have a great time. The bottom line is that you can still have fun on a budget. Plus, it starts to rub off on your friends and their lifestyle starts to shift too.

Weekly Challenge #1

Answer the following questions:

1. How much do you spend each month on entertainment?

2. How often do you go out to eat each week?

3. How much do you spend eating out each week?

4. What are five entertainment options you can refrain from doing this month to save money?

5. What could you do instead of these five things to ensure that you still have fun?

6. How much money will you save?

Please share your creative entertainment ideas with me and other readers at www.EmotionallySpent.com/community and with your friends on Facebook, Twitter or Instagram using the handle @EmotionallySpent.

Notes

Daily Spending

Monday

1. After the weekend, I feel _____ because _____.

2. My goal for this week is _____.

3. Today I am thankful for _____.

4. Today I am frustrated with _____.

Today I Feel:

Notes

Daily Spending

Tuesday

1. What was hard about today?

2. My goal for tomorrow is _____.

3. What items did you purchase today?

4. I can save money if _____.

Today I Feel:

Notes

Daily Spending

Wednesday

1. I saved _____ today because I chose not to buy _____.

2. I wish I could buy _____.

3. I am worried about _____.

4. I am hopeful about _____.

Today I Feel:

Notes

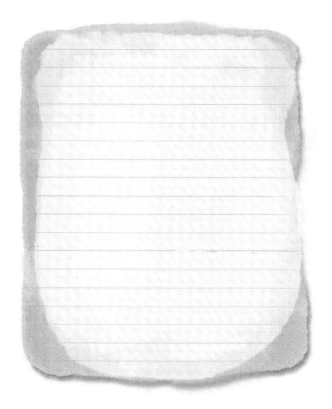

Daily Spending

Cash	Debit	Credit	Total Daily Spending

Thursday

1.   _____ made me feel happy today.

2.   I am feeling jealous of _____ today.

3.   _____ is motivating me.

4.   I have a bad habit of _____.

Today I Feel:

Notes

Daily Spending

Friday

1. I want to buy _____ this weekend.

2. How do you feel about your financial situation today?

3. What are you proud of yourself for today?

4. What is your hope for the weekend?

Today I Feel:

Notes

Daily Spending

Saturday

1. What is something you did that you are proud of this week?

2. Is there something you could have done better this week?

3. Overall, how do you feel about your financial journey so far?

4. One way I can save money this week is _____.

Today I Feel:

Notes

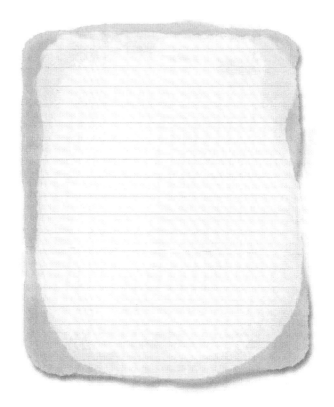

Daily Spending

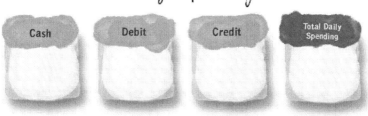

Cash	Debit	Credit	Total Daily Spending

Sunday

1. My main frustrations from last week are _____.

2. Write out your celebrations from last week.

3. I am feeling optimistic about _____.

4. This week I am willing to give up _____ to save _____.

Today I Feel:

Weekly Wrap-Up

1. The following bills are due this coming week.

2. I get paid _____ this week.

3. My goals for this coming week are _____.

4. How did you create and implement an entertainment budget?

5. Of the five things you listed in this week's challenge, what was the hardest to give up? Why?

Monthly Check-In

1. List the bills that are due this month.

2. I am getting paid _____ this month.

3. My goal is to pay off _____ debt this month.

4. This month, I am willing to give up _____ to save _____.

5. If I did _____ instead of _____ I could save _____.

6. My goals for this month are _____

Congratulations

How do you feel? You completed *Emotionally Spent!* Do you feel lighter? I hope so! I wish I was sitting across from you right now so we could smile while we talk about all your successes and shed tears over your challenges. Since I can't be there with you, is there a person with whom you can share your experience with? Your spouse, a friend, a family member, or maybe even a stranger?

My hope is that you are twelve weeks closer to your financial goals as well as equipped to explore your emotions with pen and paper. Now that you have completed *Emotionally Spent*, your work is not done. Keep journaling, don't stop now. I still use my journal as a resource to help me through the ups and downs of life.

We all have such a unique journey in life and I am so thankful you allowed me to be a part of yours. If you need additional resources please visit me at www.EmotionallySpent.com and check out my free downloads as well as other products.

Please share your *Emotionally Spent* journaling success with me and other readers at www.EmotionallySpent.com/community and with your friends on Facebook, Twitter or Instagram using the handle @EmotionallySpent.

Send me an email at Lindsay@EmotionallySpent.com to share your success as well as let me know what additional resources you need.

Want to do it again? Order another copy of this 90-day guided journal at www.EmotionallySpent.com/purchase.

Please Help!

Thank You For Reading My Book

I look forward to hearing your feedback. Please leave me a
helpful review on Amazon letting me know what you thought of
Emotionally Spent.

Thank you!!

Lindsay Snowden

84832834R00135